GOAT-FOOTED GODS

Books by Kathleen Driskell

Laughing Sickness
High Horse: Contemporary Writing by the MFA Faculty of Spalding University (co-editor with Sena Jeter Naslund)
Seed Across Snow
Peck and Pock: A Graphic Poem (illustrated by AJ Reinhart)
Next Door to the Dead: Poems
Blue Etiquette
Creativity & Compassion: Spalding Writers Celebrate Twenty Years (co-editor with Katy Yocom)
The Vine Temple

GOAT-FOOTED GODS

Kathleen Driskell

Carnegie Mellon University Press
Pittsburgh 2025

Acknowledgments

I want to thank the editors of the following magazines where these poems, sometimes in different versions, were first published.

Appalachian Review: "Blue Collar to Middle Class," "Tiara," "Jewish Cemetery, Prague," "River Walk in Winter," and "Psalm for the Heretic"
The Louisville Review: "Promise" and "Blake Looking Through Trees"
The New Yorker: "Poem for Grown Children"
Red Tree Review: "Pastoral" and "Praise for the Rabbi Who Lived Long Ago"
Still: The Journal: "Six Hours Lost, Land Between the Lakes," "After the Fall," and "The Trestle Is Haunted"
Symposeum: "Synonyms" and "Resurrection"
Water-Stone Review: "Collapse"
Women Speak: An Anthology of the Appalachian Women's Project: "Homegoing, West Virginia," "Study on the Indigo Bunting Preening in the Beech Tree," and "Fairest of All"

A number of these poems were first published, sometimes in slightly different versions, in *The Vine Temple*, published in the Cox Family Chapbook Series from Carnegie Mellon University Press.

I am grateful to Gerald Constanzo, founding publisher of Carnegie Mellon University Press, for his encouragement and support of my work. It has been a pleasure to work again with Production Coordinator, Connie Amoroso, and Senior Editor, Cynthia Lamb, at Carnegie Mellon. They're a wonder. My colleagues at the Sena Jeter Naslund-Karen Mann Graduate School of Writing are an ongoing source of inspiration and support. For their encouragement with these poems, I especially want to thank these friends, all members of our Spalding University MFA family: Lynnell Edwards, Silas House, Jason Howard, Ellyn Lichvar, Karen Mann, Andrew Najberg, Katerina Stoykova, and Katy Yocom. And I thank, too, Leigh Bullock, James Gottuso, and Keith Hall for their steadfast encouragement and their enduring friendships.

I am grateful, also, to the Hermitage Artist Retreat which allowed me time and shelter to write many of these poems.

Terry, Wyatt, Quinn, Vincent, Kaci, and, now, little August, are always at the heart of my work.

Book design by Anna Cappella

Library of Congress Control Number 2024942093
ISBN 978-0-88748-708-8

Printed and bound in the United States of America

10 9 8 7 6 5 4 3 2

for Quinn

"Despite the warning signs and a tall fence that surrounds the trestle, Pope Creek has had several accidents and deaths, some possibly related to looking for the Goatman. . . . this satyr holds the tragic distinction of being one of the most dangerous mythical animals in North America."

—*The Washington Post*, April 26, 2016

"A fifteen-year-old girl dies in yet another train accident on the Pope Lick trestle"

—headline, *Louisville Courier-Journal*, May 28, 2019

"Someone needs to go down their [sic] and shove that axe up his goat a** lol."

—post, Pope Lick Monster's Facebook page

"The lust of the *goat* is the bounty of God.
The wrath of the lion is the wisdom of God."

—William Blake, *The Marriage of Heaven and Hell*

Contents

Temple

You see your own eye
in the center of
the crow poison's
blossom.

On the surface
of the quiet pond,
articulated bugs create

circles of thought. There
in the woods, grapevines
twist into a temple.

The darkness
has grown you a door.
Walk through:

I.

Goat-Footed God

When you were born, your mother held you up
for all to admire, your little horns, your face full of soft fur,
your tiny hooves. Oh, the way you babbled and bahhed

when tickled by Zeus. He named you Pan
because you were loved by all. And now we've driven away
every one of your gods, left you without brothers, sisters,

no shepherds to look after, no flocks, no friends to call you
to play your pipes. You weren't made for this
world, yet here you are.

Six Hours Lost, Land Between the Lakes

Long after dark had fallen
and the trail left behind,

long after the dog I had chased
into the unfamiliar woods

disappeared, she long gone into oaks
and hickory and brush—and likely

back asleep on the porch
of my new boyfriend's cabin—

I saw a fire in the distance
and walked toward it. There

in their camp, orange light flashing
across their rough bearded faces,

creased in dirt, unruly feral hair,
tin cups in grimy hands

like that movie. Relaxing, they
mocked and jabbed at each other,

after a long day of timbering.
Nearly all jumped up when

I wandered in, but the youngest, a teenager,
stayed seated, continued pawing

at the ground with a hatchet
while I spoke, as if he were embarrassed.

I was about his age and pretty enough, if
that ever matters, and alone

in the woods, completely soaked
in fear, finding no real relief

in discovering their camp.
I counted quickly. There

were eight of them. Their eyes
as astonished as mine

that we were there, together,
miles away from everyone and

everything in the middle
of the night woods. They huddled

a few moments, looking over
to eye me and then back to hushed talk.

Finally, two set down their whiskeys.
It had been determined. They would be the ones

to drive me back. The drive was quiet
but for me in the middle of the cab,

pointing out turns. When I stumbled
from the old logging truck

into the washing blue lights
of the sheriff's and deputy's cars,

I rushed into the arms of a man I would
date for only a few more weeks.

It's good to remember this kindness of men,
especially in the times we are living.

Remembering the Louisville Bussing Riots

At one side of Dixie Highway, standing
in the grass, white women, mothers and
daughters and sisters, their faces twisted,
expectorating saliva caught in newspaper

photographs like the crystal drops
of chandeliers. My memory is full
of sound as well, returning hisses, sticks
on a snare drum, or a radio that's lost its channel.

But the sound, too, of bus wheels rolling
over crushed glass, as the students advanced
slowly into dangerous foreign territory,
the parking lot of what had always been,
until then, a high school for whites only.

Confederate Cross

Gone missing from Peewee Valley's
Confederate Cemetery were the young men
from our county killed in action, bodies
abandoned on the blood field, or those
who died from the bubbling green infections
ravaging camp hospitals far from
their Kentucky homes. Most young as the kids

being bussed from the inner city, all eyes
caught in the frames of bus windows
on a young white man, standing in the middle
of Louisville's Dixie Highway. (Dixie Die-way
we called it because of the countless crash
fatalities that had happened there.) He was
slick haired, parted hair curling around his ears,

cigarette hanging on lip. They watched him as
he lunged, again and again, thrusting
a flag pole with a Confederate Cross sagging
from it as if he were running into battle,
as if he wanted nothing more than to impale
each of the kids on the bus upon his bloody

shish kebab. As a kid, when I saw a car with
a Confederate flag bumper sticker, my first
thought, I admit, was redneck, not bigot.

Sulky Achilles

That's him over there—
alone, on his haunches
next to the campfire,
playing with a stick,
stirring sparks into
the hateful sky. "Fuck
Agamemnon," he mutters,
relicking his paw. He's
withdrawn and mopey,
grumpy over a girl—
he stole her first, gods
dammit. Behind him,
his buddies, faces fear
filled and green, clank
swords with the enemy
on the wine-colored fields
of Troy. He shrugs. He's
just not feeling the fury,
though wrath has always
been his gift, his thing.
And he'll unfurl it
without mercy on Hector,
and Andromache, and
Priam, and so on, he will,
but that's later. Right now,
he's promising himself,
he'll never be dumb enough
to drop his armor again. Go
big or go home, *amirite*?

After the Fall

At the park path near my home, my dog
stops always to sniff around her makeshift memorial,

a plastic wreath, a laminated poster with her photo,
at the foot of the train trestle from which she fell.

I look up 90 feet towering over, the equivalent
of falling from a building with eight floors.

Each time I pass by I wonder what in the world
could have urged her onto the tracks that night?

What dare? What thing was she looking for,
and did she find it before she heard the whistle?

Had she not stepped onto the trestle that evening,
had the train not been coming, perhaps she'd be

living in a dorm that high. There's a tower like that
at the university my daughter attended. Or the girl might be

working in an office building.
When time for her break,
she pushes back from her metal desk, catches a glimpse

down eight stories to the street below, all busyness
stopped for a moment at the red light, the delivery trucks

idling, the bicyclists balancing, keen
to wheel on. Perhaps forehead on cold glass,

she shudders, feeling a little dizzy. What might that
fall be like? At whose feet might she land before?

Someone hurrying home with a birthday cake
with blue icing or a bouquet of hydrangeas?

And what of their celebrations then?
We hear the sirens while out on

the screened porch, rosé wine in hand
on a warm Saturday night, dog curled

at our feet, when in a fallow field
beneath the trestle, the policewoman,

our neighbor, with teenagers of her own
at home (or so she thinks), walks toward

a patch of crushed blond grass. In
the byline of the newspaper article, the next

day I read the name of my student.
She's the reporter called to talk to witnesses:

she makes notes, standing beside the stream
that has always run under the trestle. A slow

rain begins to pock the water. We hear it,
too, striking our porch's red metal roof.

The Trestle Is Haunted

The trestle is haunted by a Goat-
man. He is not carrying a bible,
nor any sacred book, nor is he
wearing a priest's collar. He's not
wearing clothes at all, his eyes are
not blue like Jesus', he has no hair
though he is covered in fur, and
gnats circle his head and horns
like a gnarly halo. Some say he swings
a bloody axe. Have you seen a photo
of goats sleeping in trees? Or the video
of a goat walking upright through
the streets of India? Like a man? Then
you may be able to see what is not there,
too. At the trestle. What is not there is
what'll kill you, knock you dead
into the field below. From the trestle
tall as an eight-story building, which
is also not there, but is, nonetheless,
as deadly to fall from.

Poem for Grown Children

In a poem I love, the husband slices open
a pepper to find a church,

but here at the sink I've found a house, and
inside, the rattling seeds of a chandelier.

It doesn't matter. My husband is too by himself
in the hospital, and in our home at the window I stand

alone for the first time in almost thirty years. Then,
he'd rushed out into the dark, summoned to

his father's deathbed. But I wasn't really alone.
My toddler son slept, his mouth slightly open

and red and wet inside like a fledgling's,
my daughter grew within me, close

as a locket on a chain. When my husband returned,
I remember he talked of the rattle. The death rattle.

The children are now inside their own homes
asleep, curled around their beloveds. But all so young

yet, they do not think we will ever die.
In their garden beds, if they are dreaming of seeds

and light, they are dreaming of little blazes
growing hotter. They are not dreaming of wind

and flickering. And, certainly, they are not
dreaming of smoke.

Hymn of the Goatman No. 1: Halloo, I'm Up Here, Cupped Tenderly

Halloo, I'm up here, cupped tenderly
in the arms of my beloved sycamore tree,
the bees and sun waking me as they wake,
calling me down to the burbling love
of my creek, sometimes shallow and blue,
moving over both the creamy river gravel
and smooth slabs of limestone, sometimes
deep and green and opaque. I walk there
for my morning offices, I walk upon paths
I've traced with my fellow fauna, deer mostly,
but sometimes the waddling woodchuck
and a dashing snake. On either side of me,
higher than the horns on my head, sedge
is beginning to winter, its mauve feathery
fingers reaching out to tickle, and
goldenrod, too, and thorny thistle gone so
purple this time of year. Oh, glorious world,
oh, world wondrous, what creature or god
needs heaven with your bright yellow stars
of tickseed lighting my way to cool waters,
full of gentle fish, the blue gill, rainbow
darters, rainbow trout. If I wait here
long enough, the entire world will drift by.

Orthodoxy

Why come hunting other gods,
when you have a perfect
good god of your own?

Luck

Your father and I said nothing
as we drove an hour to the hospital:

what could be said but small prayers
to gods we do not believe in. And

if we did mumble prayers, what images
of comfort could they offer? Yesterday,

I remember thinking we were so lucky.
I remember thinking that felt like a curse.

Moped

She's down the hall on the MRI table
when he's wheeled into the emergency
room bay and the nurses pull
the thin yellow curtains around him—
as if that offers any privacy. I hear
him cry out, groaning
as the orderlies lift him onto the bed.
Forty minutes ago, he was a boy
on a moped buzzing home from
his dishwashing job. The emergency
room is a strange place. Not at all
what I'd thought. There's no urgency
here, only what seems like nonchalance—
and laughing. So much laughing. And,
shouting. The nurses and doctors and orderlies
speak to the damaged, as if we're
underwater. And so how can I help
but hear it all, what has happened
to the boy, a shattered leg
they are trying to save, his whimpering,
his calling out for his mother?
They yell that they're going to have to
put him in traction, and he must hold
still for the drill. *Do you understand?*
Can you hear me? Can you hear
me? Can you hold still? They take
his whimpering for a yes, and why
wouldn't they? Here, we're all yielding,
none of us yet understanding
what we're about to surrender.

Blake Looking Through Trees

I regret that I did not take you out
into the backyard in late spring,
in midmorning, a tattered old tree
of paradise quilt folded under my arm,
until I unfurled it, allowing it to waft
to the grass, settling like a lumpy square,
and that we didn't lay there until the sun
broke through a green hawthorne's leafy
crown, filling it with flickering light.
I would have told you then about Blake
and how as a child he hiked beyond
the busy London streets, slimy and
fouled by horses and drunks, how
he lay recumbent, alone for hours,
under glorious trees like these, imagining
that the winking lights were angels,
his angels, come to reveal themselves.
Knowing myself, I might have said
to you I do not believe in angels, nor
God—nor anything else supernatural.
But I hope I would have urged you
to see whatever you might see, my
darlings, to believe whatever you
might need or even want to believe.

II.

Hymn of the Goatman No. 2: I Squat at the Waterside with a Deer Mother

I squat at the waterside with a deer mother,
velvety soft, her ears twitching. I nod to her,
and she nudges her fawn to drink. My hooves sink
slightly in the pebbles and soft mud at the bank
and water rushes in to fill their cups. Oh, joy!
The river is playing with me! I cup my hands
and fill them, too, and drink deep and splash
to clean my furry face. Then, the little birds—
I love them best. The goldfinch pairs, swoop,
circling around me as if they are weaving
a ribbon through the edge of a woodland basket—
trying to hold my happiness, my celebratory
ablutions. Then, come, too, the little sparrows
the birds your new god loves as well as I love.
They swirl around my head, making a wreath
for me. Look at my soft fine crown of feathers!

Promise

The gods say *c'mon*,
we're offering you life
everlasting, but I'd rather
have hubris, rancor,

a greasy pork chop,
regular old smut,
a jug full of green
wine instead of
a very good glass

of claret with its nose
full of cherry and black
dirt. Sure. I know
what's good for me,

but I don't want it.
They shrug, say okay,
feels, though, like we ought to
give you some-

thing. They glance around.
Well, there's this,
they say, it's not much
to look at but here
go ahead and take it
anyway, take this bruised
old boot, mortality.

Two Queens, Ancient History

The list of war gods is long, Ares,
of course, and his sitcom-trope-twin Mars,

but, also, Great Gish and Kartikeya and
Zhou Lang. The list goes on and on . . . and

there are goddesses, too, Minerva and Diana,
and Nike and Shaushka, but women, just

women, we mere mortals, are etched into
the bellies of black ewers as weakling

handwringers. Or we're captured in epics
as wailing grace notes, gnashing our teeth

as we toddle over the battlefield, draped shadows
searching for the mutilated corpses of our sons.

Yet, in sixth-century Europe, or what we think of
as Europe, now that men have drawn maps

with solid lines, two women, two mothers,
flesh and blood queens Brunhild and Fredegund

were as ruthless and hard-nosed, as hard-hearted,
as Shiva and Yahweh. Fredegund shivved two

husbands, her arch femme enemy Brunhild's,
but, also, her very own. That dirty double-crosser.

And Brunhild never hesitated after her
husband's death. She held up his glittering shield

like a lantern, commanding her army to torch
all, and they did. Devotedly. As if she were a king.

Entire villages transformed into funnels of dark
smoke churning in the sky. History wants us

to know, though (to make sure we know), it wasn't
for power that Fredegund and Brunhild plundered

and killed: it was for their children, future kings
and queens, for certain, but still their children—

and so many children!—babes they'd suckled
in royal beds curtained with heavy tapestries,

babes they'd lifted from bath water and groomed,
gently pulling shell combs through soft lank curls,

babies that sat in their laps, being fed sweetmeats
to keep them quiet as cats. But no one remembers

the names of Brunhild's or Fredegund's children.
Not really. Nor would we, I dare say, know much

of anything about Brunhild or Fredegund,
excepting that they were the kind of women

who would gamely slap the ass of a roan
just to watch it drag a yowling man over bramble

and sharp rock until only a faraway cloud of powder.
You see, or read anyway, that they were the kind

of women who'd put two fingers in their mouths
and whistle, calling back the huffing horse to satisfy

themselves that what remained of what had been
a man was now nothing but bone and gristle.

Achilles Was a Schlub

Captain-quarterback of
the football team. Blond
as Adonis, chased by pretty girls
smart enough to know better.

Apple of his mother's eye,
but even immortals can't keep
their demigod boys safe,
especially from themselves.

Achilles burns rubber out of
the parking lot after the big game.
They'd have won for sure
if that fucker Hermes just once
could hold onto the ball.

Best thing Achilles ever did
was put his foot down as he took
dead man's curve, his car
plunging over the embankment,
his head forever full of yellow hair.

Tiara

As the Homecoming King escorted Brenda
across our football field, all heads, in unison,
turned from looking at her to Mr. Rausch,
our biology teacher, who sat with his wife
in the bleachers, his two little kids merrily
throwing popcorn at each other, laughing
and swinging their feet wildly.

Mrs. Rausch was so dour looking, so rumpled,
her hairdo a frizzy salon-frosted wedge,
that I'm sure most thought *well no wonder*
as we compared her to the beaming Miss
Oldham County Homecoming 1976. There
were insects whining in the halo of
the field's floodlights, but Brenda, her tiara,
her blue sateen gown with its princess
neckline, twinkled sweetly down below.

Tropical Fred

All long morning the little blue beach
house shook and heaved and creaked,

        and by noon the ocean had advanced,
        roaring up until it washed under the stilts,

and we could feel it swirling underneath
our feet as we made ham and pickle

        sandwiches in the kitchen. Quietly, we sat
        at the table eating, picking at a puzzle,

feeling the rowdy waves push and suck themselves
back into the gray immensity

        of water and sky. Out front, the red
        beach warning flag blew, beating so hard

we heard it through the thin windows.
Palm fronds flew by the windows, giving

        a start as they swept past like drunken witches
        on broomsticks. It wasn't a hurricane. Only,

a tropical storm. And we had been warned,
yet we threw our suitcases into the car anyway

        and drove down. It had been nearly a year
        since my daughter was hurt. We had only

a few more months, the neurosurgeon said,
so casually, to watch her recover fully, if

        she were going to. For days, I had watched her
        grab hold of the pier's handrail and climb

down to the ocean like a young child. One
foot on the step, followed by the other,

    steady on, finding her balance, then one
    foot followed by the other. Following her

to the water's edge, carrying things
she used to carry for herself, I slogged through

    the sand, and my calves burned, but
    I was making the best, you know, and so said cheerfully,

"great workout for our legs, right?"
and she looked back at me,

    her long curly hair blowing in strands across her
    face, smiling as she had when a teen,

when I tried to say something about some
thing. If you've mothered teens, you know

    the look.
        She fretted, wadded up
    her napkin, threw it on her plate, dumped

a triangle of sandwich I had just cut
for her and a pile of orange chips

    we bought only when at the beach.

    I was going to tell you the chips rattled

like seashells as they went into the trash,
but thought better of it.

Contranyms

Pan means all, after all, all
things to all men, that horny god
thrashing through the woods,

chasing maenads, his phallus fully
erect. But, isn't he also a defender
of nature, of all little wooly creatures,

moles and voles, alike, and beetles. And
coyotes and bobcats, all that make forest
noise to raise the goose flesh . . .

He's all we ever wanted him to be
and all we ever never wanted—
or so we say. For a short while

he was both Satan and Christ.
Hard to believe, when we see Preacher
so worked up at the pulpit, a drop

of sweat about to fall from
his nose. He's afraid and so wants us
to be afraid, to be panicked

about everything the Goatman,
this shape-shifter, has to offer
boys and girls, his flock.

Won't Preacher ever understand
that once this silly god means everything,
he means nothing particular at all?

Pathetic Fallacy

I'm buttering dry toast,
when agitation catches my eye.
Violently fluttering, the dove descends,
dun wings outstretched, less like
an angel, more like a superhero, dropping
awkwardly onto the windowsill feeder
as if he's the Redemption Spawn landing
with a thud into a street fight of goons.
But dumb, too. He knows he's a poser.
When he folds his wings, he's exposed as
ridiculously potbellied, his breast feathers
sullied, rumpled—in no way white
as his posh cousins shot into the air
at weddings. His feathers more like the gray-
purple that swirls through a puddle of gasoline.
Lovely in its own spoiled way, I suppose, if
I'm being fair, but I don't want to be fair,
because of the way his black eyes eye me,
sizing me up, judging me lacking, as
his head turns to this side and that,
pretending he's just ogling my toast.

Mother, Visiting

She's here for a week, in this house
where my husband and I have lived
for nearly thirty years, and not far from

where she used to live, just down
the road, so close we drove back
and forth sometimes several times a day

to drop off the kids, or feed each other's dogs
when away. Yet, now, looking around, she says
how much she has always loved living

in this home—though, odd, she doesn't
remember choosing all the furniture.
She says she must have been in a mood

when she bought those ugly rugs. She wishes
she'd spent more on the drapes, and
in the future, she has to do a better job

of keeping house. Look at all those
cobwebs, she says, pointing into
the tall corners of my dining room.

It takes me a moment to see them.
I have to take a step to the side and,
then, yes, those gossamer strands

like garland, draped from one wall to
the other, shimmering
in the sunlight of late day.

As she has so many other times,
in this gesture, she claims my failing
as her own. But, also, my glories.

Through Water

Shed your blue shoes and leave
them with the book about the sad
woman on the blanket in the sand.

See your feet walking through water,
your toenails, just painted purple.
See the silver school of slim fish,

mullet catching light as they shoot by.
Pull your legs through the weight
and suck of waves rocking

to and from. Turn from the horizon.
Look back at the weathered house
on stilts, the bright towels pink, lime,

and red, like flags flapping from the rail,
flags of countries you've decided not
to visit. There, too, your daughter

holds the baby and waves, gesturing
wildly as if she's the one on the deck
of a steamship puffing away from the pier.

Walk in the Graveyard with My Mother

On her visit, my eighty-year-old mother
wants to walk among the old
headstones of the small graveyard
next to our home. She wants to see

if she remembers any of the names
of those buried there, though no one
next door is any of our kin, and her
memory has been shot for years.

Still, she leads her little graying dog
through the grass, and I follow close by.
I say, look here. This is the oldest grave,
and stoop to pull the long grass

and wild carrot nearly obscuring
the blunted stone of Alpha Beta
Blankenbaker, Infant, 1857, alone,
abandoned here a hundred or more

years. I'm trying to recall, my mother
says, which side of the family
she comes from. On this earth, at this
moment, it feels as if we, two,

are the only ones alive who know that
tiny Alpha Beta Blankenbaker
was in our world, if only for a day. That
she existed. She's from our side, I say.

Study on Lilac Bush to the Right of Our Porch

The weakened lilac is sorely
in need of pruning, the horticulturist

friend has admonished. Otherwise,
the dead knotted wood will sway

and clack and rub against the green
wood—and worse will mar future

blooms. Further, I should be advised
that the best time for pruning

is just after blossoming, after
the bumblebees have glugged

all that can be glugged from its purple
spires. He stooped, showing me how far

he'd cut back the tree if it were his.
What's this, he laughed and held out

his palm. A tiny firetruck, hidden
for decades in the grass

at the lilac's brushy feet. Whom
among us, I wonder, that we'd favor,

anyway, would cut that old lilac
back to near nothingness?

Passing Bells

They were rung in small towns
across America to let all know
a neighbor had passed, a chiming
signal for us to pause chores
and bow heads for a moment
before returning to our work.

And, then, we did turn back to the day-
to-day, though some of us continued
to shoulder thoughts of those whom
without any church notice had carried
their own bones quietly through
the dark door of the woods.

Confederate Cemetery

I learned from the historic plaque
that the veterans buried in the small
section had not died as young men
in battle, but had succumbed nearby
in the Old Confederate Home
with gingerbread trim around its wide porch.
There, as kids like me pedaled past
on our way to the store to buy Bazooka,
death had come a calling.

Something I'd read must have helped me
realize the bones under my feet were
on the wrong side of it all, how else
would I have known, along with the slurs
at the dinner table, my neighborhood,
sprung up recently as a white asylum
from school desegregation, that things
were not as they said they were?

Still, in a house filled with shouting
and threats and heaved plates (the offending
meatloaf sliding down the wall, leaving
a wet smear as if a traitor had just been
executed in our kitchen), I solaced in
the tidiness, the unyielding order of those
markers, government issued, and aligned
painstakingly within that half acre.

Statuary

If both front feet of a horse
are reared in a statue, the rider
is presumed killed in battle.

If one front hoof is raised, the rider
is presumed wounded in battle.

If all four horse hooves stand firmly
on the ground, the rider died a natural death,
say in his sleep at the Old Confederate Home,
across the fence and down the road.

If a soldier limping toward home,
ends up dying alone in the brush,
there is no horse, no statue.

In Winter We See It All

When we walk the dog
in winter, the weather is cold and brittle,
but we can see the bones of trees,
the white-limbed sycamores I find
so thrilling—but, too, the shaggy bark
peeling from the hickories.
We point out the mistletoe
and squirrel nests, those exalted
nests of owls, stop to stand under
the red-tailed hawk, just above, so
close we see his cruel talons curled
around the knotty limb of
a crabapple tree. Then a little
Kentucky bluebird swoops by,
turns our heads, its orange belly
blush, a jolt of color, unexpected
here, so easy to follow, flying over
the brown and mauve brickle field.
We watch him perch atop the feathery
sedge, are still wondering what
he's doing here, now, we mean,
in winter, when we hear whooshing
wings—the hawk come hunting.

A Child in Mexico

Nearly his entire life, my husband
had been afraid of needles
until his cancer became the cure
for his phobia. When he recalls
being taken to the edge of the Mexican
jungle, carried into the old nurse's
rusty travel trailer, held tight, against
squirming, so that her long needle
might jab him with penicillin, each day
for seven days, now, he's able to
step from the trailer, look up to see
the giant gray iguana asleep upon a tree
branch, efflorescent with white orchids.

Afterwinter

a period of unseasonably cold or bad weather when spring is expected

More a nuisance really, that sharp chill
that interrupts the first warm days of mid-March.

To complain too much is to be a child—to
want what you want when you want it—

the grown you knows perfectly well patience
will bring the lilac blossoms, then the bees.

Unless you believe what you read. That one
day we'll be nostalgic for any bit of winter,

that quiet nothingness of snow falling or ping of sleet

III.

Collapse

A sunny afternoon, sugar maple leaves
beginning to go ochre and salmon, and
speckling with brown spots, but it's only
September, so most still cling to the trees.

A month later, as we go in and out of
the hospital parking garage, dried leaves
swirl around our feet and look a lot like
schools of goldfish whirling in eddies of air—

but that day, the day, on the branches
the leaves quiver as if warning what's to come,
that creak, that crackle, an almost imperceptible
moan, slight stirrings of noise heard first in

underground tunnels by worms and curled grubs
the color of old teeth, the Earth beginning
to shake, rumble, and quake; then, things activate,
begin to shift and skitter, the stainless

steel grill is rocking across the gray boards
of the deck, beer bottles slide upon the glass
top table, leaving slimy trails like snails
and all is falling, things and people—my

daughter sliding from her patio chair,
then completely airborne, like that flight
attendant—the news reported her sucked
out of the plane's emergency door at

30,000 feet, but aren't there just so
many feet to fall here, twenty, perhaps
less? Isn't hurt proportionate to the
distance one falls? But now she's hit the ground,

things bouncing around her, that grill,
the weight of a small car, come to rest only
a foot from her spilled out of the chair, and splayed
on the ground—here come other things as well,

a plastic wine glass with pink silly daisies,
its pinot grigio expelled in a plume
as if from a fancy fountain in Las Vegas,
the glass top of the table shattering,

shards exploding and then caught, hovering,
sparkling in the afternoon sun. Stunning.
Might that be the last thing she ever sees,
those hundreds of crystal teardrops tinkling

in the light above her? Tinkling against
the sky of speckled leaves, the sunlight setting
all alight as in Blake's vision? Why didn't I
teach her about Blake and trees and angels?

Later, when I see her imaging, the shards
of white bone, her shattered T-12, my eyes
will reiterate all of this. But, then,
they fall, too, all teardrops fall noiselessly,

among the blades of grass. In the ER,
I will find little spears of glass stuck in her
scalp as I smooth her hair, watch the nurse
inject the morphine and follow it

journeying with slippery ease through her
IV tube and into the needle taped
to the back of her purpling hand. Hurt must be
proportionate, I litany all night,

as if I am a god and have power
to make anything at all true, and all
night, as the nurses come and go, and for days
afterward, weeks, I shove her away from

me. Attendant. Still dropping. Tumbling
violently through the sky toward
a field of deep blue snow.

Listing

After the accident—I should say *her*
accident—I stood by her bed all night

and pulled twigs and bits of dried leaves
from her curly brown hair, and sat in a hard chair,

in vigil, watched as the aides in bright blue scrubs
wheeled her bed out of the emergency room bay

again, and again, and down the narrow hall, where,
though the door was closed, I heard her scream

each time they lifted her onto the table
for another MRI, and I watched the clock

for morphine, and overnight, I watched
the clock in wait for the neurosurgeon

to wake from his soft bed, for his coffee
to finish dripping into a pot, for him

to kiss his children goodbye as they ran off
to the school bus, for his finger to wheel

through his texts—willed him to see
that it was she who needed him most,

very first that morning.
I waited and ticked down the list

of things I would give up for her, and
even after I got to *walking,* I went on.

Military Headstones

On military headstones,
at the top, often a Christian cross
is incised into the gray granite,
and if you squint your eyes you see
cross, cross, cross, cross, cross, all
calling, *come on across*, and so on.

Benediction

Why pray you find me crouched just
beyond the path's blurred edge, that I'll reach out
to catch somebody with my claws? Or that
my green eyes will lure them onto the train
tracks? I see all, after all, *your claws*, you

boys; you sharpen them during Sunday
prayer services, mumble amen and
then drive out to the trestle, park under
its ruined temple with your pals and a couple of
girls, hoping to put your hands up their skirts,

but you always pull back, don't you, as if
what you touch has burned? Remembering
the preacher's words, you zip up, stomp away,
blind and dumb with your stunted want and gall,
because what you want is what you think I have.

You grumble this psalm as you cross the trestle:
the Goatman leads me to the tracks, he deafens
me to the blowing of the train, heaped with coal,
locomoting, belching black smoke, engine now
turning around the near bend, bearing on.

And you repeat it all as you sit
in the back of the police car, wan-faced,
weeping, somehow—how?—
how did you make it across while your friend lies
covered with a white sheet in a plot

surrounded by yellow tape in yonder field?
Oh, wretched mortal, you'd been
so certain your god more powerful than
me, so utterly full of white fury.
And, about your god, you were right.

Little Green Fish

When you were in his lap
and his hands slid into
your underpants,
the little one you were
was buried inside
yourself. You rocked her
coffin like a cradle
for years. Then—
who can say why
it was then, when,
when no one can ever
say why—you pulled
her out like a green fish
on a line, out came
the long string, out,
out, she slipped, wriggling,
finally, through your mouth.

Homonyms

In school. First grade perhaps? Maybe,
second. We are studying language.
Homonyms—now they are called homophones,
I think. Each child is asked to make a poster
to illustrate a pair of words that sound
the same but mean different things.

On one side of my poster board, I draw
a red and white striped ball. On the other,
the face of a child, pale, pink, eyes
squinted, tears spurting out across
the poster. Curly hair, like mine.

I shiver. What have I drawn? How
is it possible for one sound to do that,
to have one meaning that rises while
the other falls, like a schoolyard seesaw.
And this, though I knew it not
then, this metaphor for the life to come,
a seemingly bland perfect sphere, a toy,
potential for joy, watered by woe.

Burnt Orange

I don't think he actually hit her,
I learned, though, it doesn't matter
if the threat is always there. Hadn't he
reared back, hammer overhead, blue
eyes wild as Jesus's in the temple,
threatening to bash my brains in
when he'd called me down to
the basement to help him with the chore.

My crime? Standing there while he
was unable to loosen the rusted hose
from the washing machine. *Burnt orange,*
I remember thinking. I remember thinking
I will be killed in the basement of this house
where I have lived for twelve years,
with these people, but I will not flinch. And
then, of course, I did. Flinch. I mean.

Blue Collar to Middle Class

My parents aspired to climb into the middle
class and cling tight. PTA, golf scrambles,
bridge. A frothy whiskey sour, plastic pink
spear, complete with hilt, driven through
the bright maraschino cherry and an orange
slice dropped atop and floating in chipped
ice, ordered whenever out with couples
who had learned to ask for their steaks
medium rare, sneering at the sweet French
dressing the waitress rattled off with options
for tossed salads. Instead, they requested
creamy Italian, just then in vogue.

The wives pulled the cherry stems through
their teeth and shook their heads. No,
of course, they won't allow their children
to be bussed—though, they did not think
of themselves as bigots. Hadn't they just come
of age in the Age of Aquarius? Hadn't they
rolled up the carpets in their living rooms,
pushed them against the walls, and allowed
Chubby Checker to teach them how to twist?

Synonyms

Though used interchangeably, as with most
synonyms there is a denotative
as well as a connotative difference
between a *graveyard* and a *cemetery.*

A graveyard rests beside a church: one
wanders from the pews and pulpit to visit
the still members of his congregation.

But one usually enters a cemetery
under a vine-covered arch, or sometimes
between pillars of brick and mortar
with carriage lights atop each.

There are gardens and religious
monuments, statues of saints,
and reflecting pools and winding paths
to be walked while introspecting, perhaps
a loose philosopher behind an old cedar.

Headstones mark the graves
of those laid to rest next to another with
whom they've likely never had a conversation,
much less an argument about Jesus,
and never will henceforth. Heaven.

Resurrection

And possibly someday my own ashes
will be scattered through the meadows
of tickseed, carrot weed, and drooping dog
hobble, Kentucky wildflowers that I love.

A speck of me might be caught in the wind
and dropped like a flea into the cupped hand
of a bellflower, falling upon a beetle that has slipped
away and fallen asleep within that blossom.

When later the beetle is eaten by the finch
I might be swooped through the blue air of summer,
riding as high as any of the orthodox resurrected.

Paradox

The ancient church seems
to be sinking, but the docent
will tell you it isn't, rather
the graveyard next to it
is rising as insects and time
churn busily, toiling to turn
all to soil.
            If one is buried
in an ancient graveyard,
paradoxically, only then is it
possible to be lowered and
lifted at the same time.

Jewish Cemetery, Prague

I learned when I visited
the Jewish cemetery in Prague,
that the dead were relegated
to one plot behind their synagogue,
so small that layering graves became
the only way to give way for the new

dead; consequently, in that graveyard
the ground provides no mossy idyll.
All appears to be erupting, the headstones,
wrecked teeth, as if the dead are struggling
to escape their coffins, as if the dead
have learned that for some
there is no place to be forgotten.

River Walk in Winter

for Claudia Emerson

All is quiet here this morning.
It's too cold and early for runners,
though their kids are already
in yellow buses on the roads over there
beyond these woods.

No one is walking a dog,
yet, despite the wind, most
dogs would be here happily.

In the year or so before she died,
when able, she'd walk in a park
along a path next to a river,

somewhat like this,
and try not to think about cells
dividing. And growing. So odd
to think of growing as a negative.
Especially now. In winter, I mean.

She was loved again.

And, she loved him.

She loved dogs, too, but she grew
so angry, she said (she needn't have,
I heard the rage in her voice),
when they came bounding toward
her off their leashes, their owners
walking casually behind,
expecting everyone to be
as delighted as they
that they owned
such marvelous creatures.

I feel compelled to defend her,
to say again that she loved dogs.

To make sure that you heard me.

She loved all animals, really.

(She loved the whole fucking world.)

So maybe it was as those dogs
bounded toward her, they made her realize
just how easily, then, she could be completely
knocked off her feet
by what she loved.

Moth

I lay on the flowered davenport, my head in her lap,
to hear her talk of the first husband who came home early
to find her suitcases and hatboxes ready at the door.

How he beat her until she lay curled like a sick old cat
on the linoleum floor of their kitchen, watching him drop
every hat she owned into a garbage can he'd set on fire.

Oh, how I loved stories like these. Like a brown moth, that
had tired of fluttering through the night, I landed, pressed
my wings against the warming glass of that kitchen door.

Morning Dew

When the morning sun spills over the tip of
the hill, the autumn meadow which had
seemed so quiet, begins to flicker with light,
acres of wrecked webs suddenly visible,

all filaments now glistening with dewed
orbs. For as far as one can see,
one village after another, sacked by
marauders, who finding nothing more
to pillage have moved on.

Here and there, a mummified fly twirls in remain,
autumn stalks, sad filaments, sad strands unloosed
and trying to break free, slight fog rising as if
from smoldering ruined ashes—and then, one
web nearly perfect, facets intact, appears like
the glorious rose window of Notre Dame.

Pastoral

On a warm day in winter, I walked
away from my unhappy flock
to skip through dried weed and

wave a wand, a stem of thorny black
locust, and then I stooped to watch a hare,
heart beating through dusky fur

and then I dipped at the brown edge
of the pond where the heron raised
its spear, victoriously piked

with a wriggling fish.
I had been gone for days
when I saw God reach through

low cloud cover, his fingers skittering
in the brush, fingers like spider legs
running this way, then that.

I watched God's fingers stop
nonchalantly to rub out something
between thumb and pinky.

He may be able to drag me
back into the fold,
but I'm not going easily.

I'm waiting, ducked under
the sumac with the ruby-beaded tips.
I'm wearing a new coat

of wooly cockles and wielding
a torch ablaze with honey
and furious bees.

Psalm for the Heretic

The lord is my shepherd
and leads me to slaughter.
Let's not pretend otherwise.
After all, my mind is
frilled with tomorrows.

Why ask me to love
the lamb seized for your
Sunday supper? Oh, god,
grant me a calendar
blank as a sheep's.

Praise for a Rabbi Who Lived Long Ago

The Roman soldiers built a pyre
of dried wood, I imagine cypress,
then dragged the old Rabbi out.

He'd been wrapped like a mummy
in a Torah scroll. Two soldiers lashed him
to the stake, then touched a blazing torch

to the wood at his feet. "What do you see?"
his followers shouted out as they stood among
a mob come to watch the old man burn.

Smoke rose and flames began to climb
though the lines of scripture. He called back:
"The parchment is burning, but the words

are flying away." Thousands of miles
from that stone piazza, more than a thousand
years later, in the tradition of another religion,

but without faith in any gods, I sit on
a beach, palms open for catching a bit of ash.

IV.

The Girl Who Became a Tree

What young woman walking by
a construction site hasn't, in that
moment, wished for a wish to
transform herself into a laurel tree?

Then, again, what woman hasn't met
a man who when coming upon a woman
transformed into a tree, thinks firstly,
yeah, boy, I'd like to climb that.

Homegoing, West Virginia

After the quick service in the funeral home,
the spluttered amens, and
folks who came up to pat
his waxy hand, and/or lay a palm upon
his hardening
cheek, we followed the hearse
onto WV-39, our purple flags fluttering
to remind us we went together.

The hearse slowed, turning onto
Panther Mountain,
and went round and round
and round and round

toward the top
where it eased to the side of the gravel road.
In a car far behind, I slid out
and was caught by
wild raspberry bushes.

In the prickly red chair before the light
of the popping coal fire, I kept my eyes
on Jesus's blue eyes
over the mantel, above a long gun,
after he'd called me to sit in his lap.
It was before dawn,
before others,
the women, of the cabin had awakened.

Now, I watched some of those same women, older
now, around me, kin, pull off
their good church shoes, reaching
into back seats to grab sneakers or slip-ons.

My grandfather's pallbearers, his
sons and sons-in-law, transferred
the casket from the hearse to
the back of a pickup truck, bulging
wheel hubs so rusted
they looked like lace
that might snag or tear our skirts.

Then, Uncle Skeeter slapped the truck's side like
a horse's ass, twice hard, and the back
tires spun a bit in the loose gravel
before grabbing, lurching forward.

Later, around a table filled with deviled eggs
and green beans with new potatoes,
they admonished me for wearing
my high heels to his graveside—see how
they'd been wholly ruined
on the mountain, sinking
deep into the moss and mud.

I chewed on a ham biscuit, a bit of pink gristle
catching in my mouth. I swallowed that
I'd come home just to delight
the man was dead, wishing only
that my heels had been able
to punch holes
through his putrescent
heart while he was yet living. Putrescent, I chewed
more on that greasy word, a word
I imagine I learned
only by leaving.

Perfect Apollo

King of the superlatives in
the high school yearbook
of the gods—best player,
best archer, best slayer,
most likely to succeed.
Jesus! We hated him,
best dancer, best writer,
blah, blah, blah, blah,
100 A-plus, grumbled
we tattooed kids,
in motorcycle jackets
and jeans, killing time
in the smoking area,
waiting for Pan and
Dionysus to get out of
detention, so we could run
off, strip down to our
nothingnesses at the edge
of the swimming hole.

Pulchritudinous

We've all known people like this,
haven't we? So clearly ugly, so cruddy
at their core, they're beautiful.
Beguiling. Bewitching. They're
the pus-filled blondes that fill
all of Patroclus's sumptuous dreams.

Supernatural

A blinking bug's green light.
A hand with knuckles articulated.
A dog you believe loves you.
A field of spiderwebs, outlined by globes
of tremulous dew, lit in the morning
sun. Four indigo buntings waiting as you come
out of the woods and into the August meadow.
Your head turning toward the gray heron's
raggedy call. The thought that everything
will be okay wrestling down
the thought that it won't.

Study on the Indigo Bunting Preening in the Beech Tree

This morning, you, dazzling
in an unexpected place,
the leafy crown of a beech tree,
sun lighting your iridescent
blue-black coat shimmery
as a tuxedo jacket worn
by a boy I hardly remember.

As I walked down the buckling
driveway behind him, catching
my high heel when he opened the door
of his father's car for me, just
the way his father had reminded
him to, then helped me tuck in
the satin edge of my skirt, romantic
as the lining in a casket, I fingered
the violet orchid corsage on my wrist
and wondered how far
I might go that night.

The next dawn, it was
birdsong that bore me back up
three concrete porch steps
to my family's house.
Glittering high heels in hand,
I stopped at the door for a moment
before walking in, thinking, then,
I'd done it, and would enter
as someone new, someone not
afraid, perhaps still broken,
but now loved.

It would take years to learn
the infinite ways
there are to be broken,
but, also, the infinite ways
to heal. It would take years,
too, to learn that you,
pocket-sized blue bird
I treasured so much, are but
one half of the pair that returns
each April to find new love.

I turn from you, your cheerful
song, to search in the trees,
I'm looking for the homely female,
common-looking as a brown wren,
snug in her open-cupped nest.
She's harder to find, but that,
too, I've learned, means she's more
likely to survive until next fall,
to lift off again, to wing to
some tropical place, navigating
her way there by the stars.

Ekphrasis

In a cave in Sulawesi,
ancient drawings of bucking buffalo
and whiskered warty pigs,
with hunters in chase.

The men have spears
and sticks but also horns
and beaks, tails and snouts, so
they are more than mere men.

They are men that can be
only imagined. Men
the cave artists provided
for our dreams.

In a cave. A beak. A horn.
Tails and snouts. Bedrock
for all religious beliefs,

among drawings of hands
reaching for something to grasp
hold of, hands that look as if
they belong to those drowning
in a blood-pigmented sea.

Kandilakia

On the steep mountain highway
to Delphi, our bus
passes a dozen or more of them
at the side of the road, little,

white-washed churches, like
birdhouses atop
poles, and reminding me of mail-
boxes back home,

memorials for those who've died
in car crashes
on hairpin turns, mainly young
men driving drunk,

pulled from wrecks with the squid
and cuttlefish stink
of fish market jobs in their
thick hair. At Delphi,

our guide will tell us we stand
at the center of the world.
We'll yell "hal-looo" to our friends
across the amphitheater,

walk the cypress-lined paths,
then, return to the busses
when we are called. On the way
down, in the falling

night, some of the little churches
now flicker with votive
lights that our guide says are
tended by mothers of the dead.

So many gods in these mountains
long ago, but only one god left now
to mind what needs tending
in this vast sore world.

Fairest of All

Two hours earlier we'd zipped
each other up, stuck bobby pins

in one another's hair, tucking them
into our special updos. We borrowed

pink cologne and rhinestone earrings
to wear. We'd lovingly stroked on blue

eye shadow and shared lipsticks,
caring nothing we said about catching

something from one another. And now
we stood together at the dark edges

of the gymnasium, a rented glitter ball
throwing sparks across the concrete block walls,

and we fidgeted, unaccustomed to our high heels,
seeing that the cutest boy in school, dark bangs

across one eye, was walking toward
us. We'd not even noticed that a moment before

he'd rolled an apple across the dance floor,
and it was now resting, bruised, at our feet.

Another Design

During this part of summer the wild pink
and white hyacinths, their dinner-plate
faces open, their yellow tongues of stamen
wagging to tempt the bees, are watchful. A heron,
neck long and curled as the hook of a hanger
holding an old gray coat, slowly
raises one leg and holds it in the air
a moment before lowering it back
into the slime of the shallow pond.
Her head cocks slightly to better eye
a small bass flicking through the murk
of pond water, the little fish hoping
to catch the circle of a dragonfly just
lighting upon the water's surface,
resting there for what the dragonfly
must presume to be but a second—

Etymology

Did you know the word *alone* means
all one? And that *only* means one-ly.

Doesn't that feel less lonely?

Bunting

A little bird that looks like
a lark and called thus,
perhaps, because of its plump rump,
the "bontin," as the Welsh

used to say when pointing to
a horse's ass, or,
after a few foamy ales,
the fat barmaid turning

away, as in look at the bontin on that
one, would you, fellas?
But also, when I turn onto
the trailhead, catch

a blue-bright bird, a newel
cap, perched, at the tip-
top of the sumac's cone, its berries
beginning to bronze—

a bounty, a gift, a favor bestowed
freely. Such goodness. Good.

This Life Is Passable

for Patricia Hudson

And here, once more for yore,
Rebecca Boone follows restless
Daniel, uprooted, walking
beside the wooden wagon

wheels turning, sometimes stopping
to bury a child on the trail
they'll never travel again.
Cheeps and tweeps and

caterwauls behind the wall of dark
trees. How many times
must she have wanted to lie down
in grave grass, let

the world pass on, or allow her
to pass on, pass away,
or maybe just pass out,
for a few moments

of peace, to lose consciousness
(or loose her
consciousness) from this world
and its abundant decay,

the wanderlust of her twitchy
husband. How strong
it must have been, her desire
to stay, to become passé.

Not a passant beast ever in
sight again. But that's not the way
the world works, is it? All keeps
passing. No wonder we drink.

More Contranyms

We live on
in the world of Babel.

So many words, perhaps
all of them, mean more
than one thing.

Some confused enough
to mean what they mean
but also their contraries.

We want out of
the language,
we're out of.

Hymn of the Goatman No. 3: I Leave the Waterside and Weave Through

I leave the waterside and weave through
the coppiced woods, where a number
of trees have two trunks emanating
from their rooted foot, twisting in embrace,
growing toward the sky, more of a miracle
than Daphne, her violent story. They are
yin and yang, the self-accepting two sides
of self. Had I been king of the gods,
and not simply regarded as a foppish prince,
I'd have waved a wand to make it all
merry. I'd have piped and danced and spread
love sparkle throughout. There'd be death,
of course—even Olympus had a flipside,
down the hill and across that steamy river,
but my god, if I were directing, the moth
would be so filled with bliss that when
it hit the web it would not panic, nor
struggle nor twist, but rather it would be
stunned in total awe of the gossamer
threads, the marvel its fellow spider had spun.
The moth would quiet, stilling its wings,
and drift off into the sweet peace of sleep,
for the time had come to sleep.

Coda

When brother Prometheus
stole fire, father
god cursed him and more,
you know, the awful bit
about that eagle and the perpetual
picking at Prometheus's
liver. Geez. Always so danged
mad, daddy-o,
and full of nerves, you old
worrywart, ever
anxious that once we wretched mortals
had fire we wouldn't need
any of you anymore.
But how in heaven
is it possible for a god
to be so wrong, so
utterly unprescient?
Your fire had shown us
that you—or
your ilk anyway—
were plenty handy.
We were sure you had lots
more tricks to teach us—
and a whole heap
more to covet.